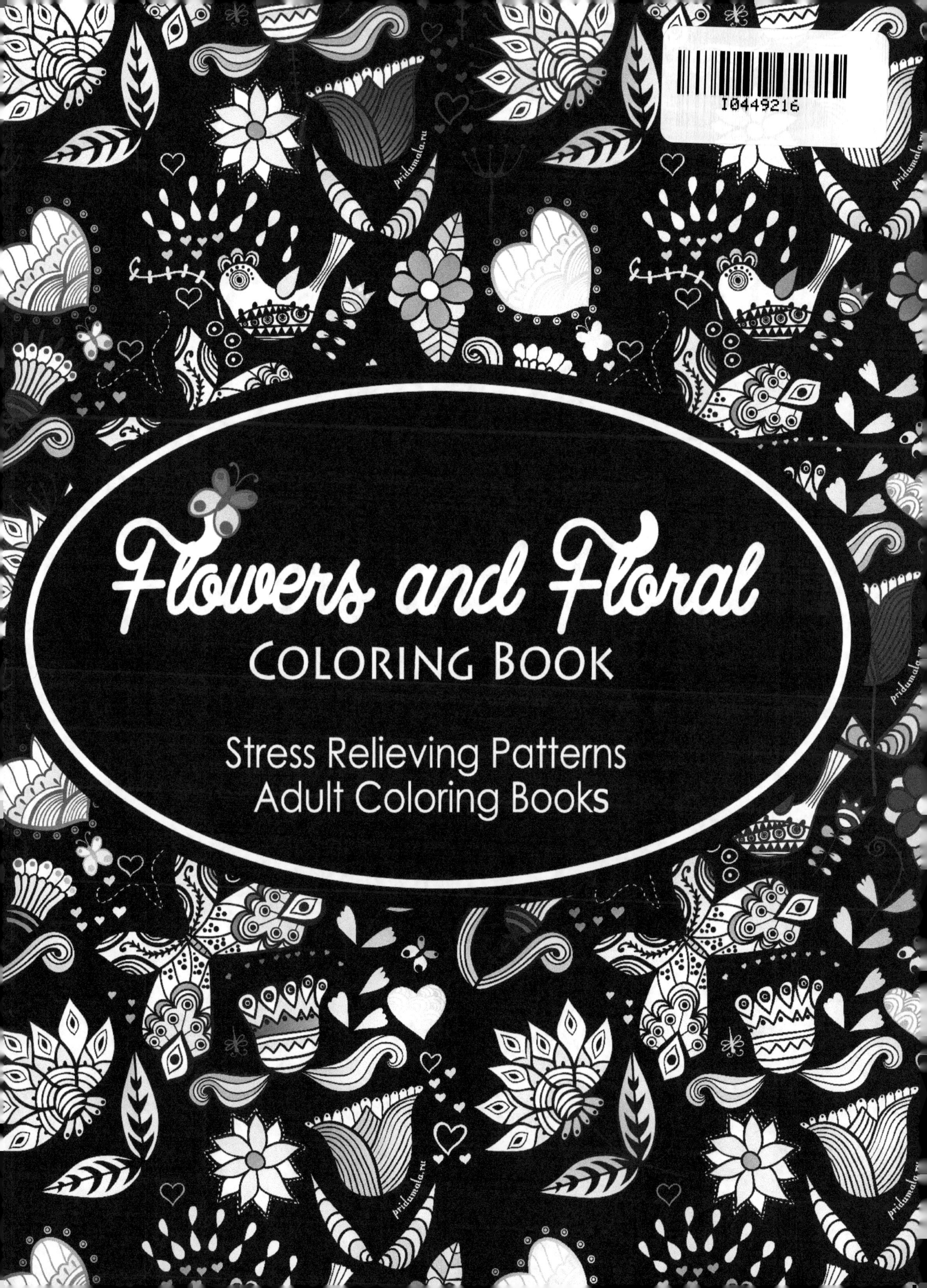

Flowers and Floral

Coloring Book

Stress Relieving Patterns
Adult Coloring Books

COLOR TEST PAGE

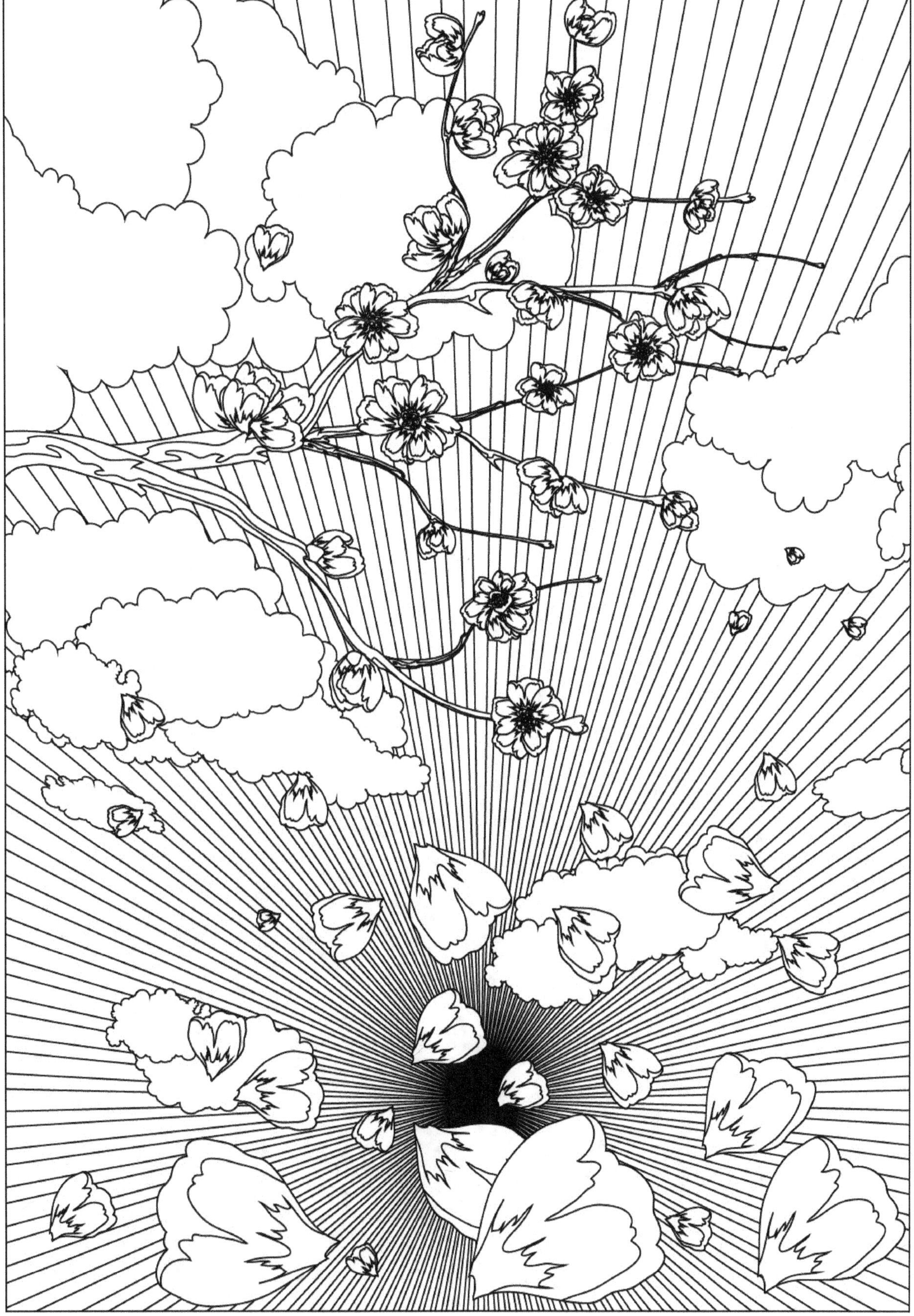

www.ingramcontent.com/pod-product-compliance
Lightning Source LLC
Chambersburg PA
CBHW052017280526
45793CB00005B/1010
9781535250658